TURBOCHARGED TRANSFORMATION

THE ULTIMATE BLUEPRINT FOR ACCELERATING GROWTH

SAGE THOMPSON

Copyright © 2024 by Sage Thompson

All rights reserved.

No part of this publication may be reproduced, distributed, or transmitted in any form or by any means, including photocopying, recording, or other electronic or mechanical methods, without the prior written permission of the publisher, except in the case of brief quotations embodied in critical reviews and certain other noncommercial uses permitted by copyright law.

The information in this book is true and complete to the best of our knowledge. All recommendations are made without guarantee on the part of the author or publisher. The author and publisher disclaim any liability in connection with the use of information

Table of contents

INTRODUCTION: BUSINESS TRANSFORMATION REQUIRES SPEED 5
    Welcome to the Next Phase of Development 5
    Why is turbocharged transformation necessary? 7

CHAPTER 1: ESTABLISHING THE BASE 15
    Comprehending Growth Dynamics 15
    Evaluating Your Present Situation 20
    Establishing High Yet Achievable Objectives 24

CHAPTER 2: STRATEGIC PLANNING 31
    Formulating a Sturdy Plan 31
    Allocating Resources for Maximum Impact 38
    Controlling and Reducing Risks 42

CHAPTER 3: SUPERIOR PERFORMANCE 51
    Putting Your Plan into Action 51
    Organizational Culture and Leadership 56
    Digital Transformation and Technology 60

CHAPTER 4: ASSESSING ACHIEVEMENT AND EXPANDING 69
    KPIs and Performance Metrics 69
    Maintaining Speed 75
    Growing Your Company 80

CONCLUSION: THE PROSPECTS FOR INCREASED DEVELOPMENT 87

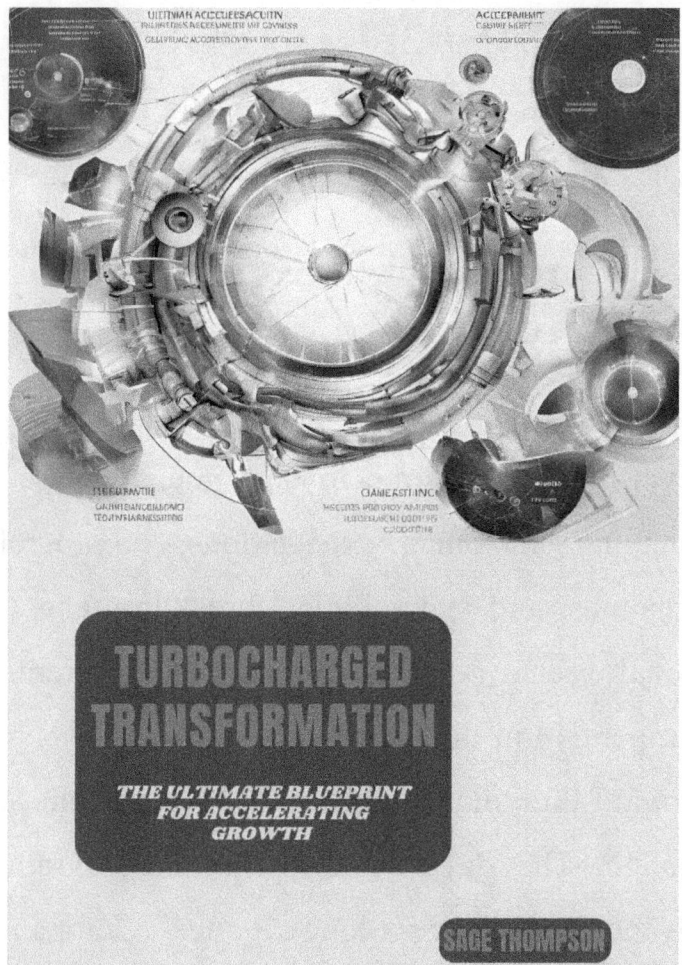

INTRODUCTION: BUSINESS TRANSFORMATION REQUIRES SPEED

Welcome to the Next Phase of Development

The rate of change is increasing at a never-before-seen rate in our time. Because of changing customer expectations, commercial dynamics, and technological breakthroughs, the global scene is always changing. To remain competitive in this new age, firms need to take a forward-thinking approach to development and change. The days of accepting little, gradual advancements are long gone. Companies nowadays must be inventive, flexible, and able to quickly adjust in order to take advantage of possibilities and reduce risks.

Greetings from the center of rapid change on this thrilling voyage. This book is your go-to resource for comprehending and putting into practice the tactics required to spur expansion and accomplish long-term success. We'll look at the ideas, strategies, and best practices that top businesses use all across the globe to improve their value propositions, change the way they operate, and break into new markets. Our objective is to offer you a thorough blueprint that you may modify to fit your particular situation, giving you the ability to confidently and clearly negotiate the intricacies of the contemporary business world.

It's critical to understand that the requirement for speed in company transformation isn't only a reaction to outside forces as we set out on this journey together. It represents a more significant, deeper change in the way we think about success and progress. It's about developing an attitude that values adaptability, encourages creativity, and accepts change. It's about realizing that in a world where change is the only constant, those who can adjust to new circumstances quickly and skillfully will prosper, while those who stubbornly adhere to the status quo will unavoidably fall behind.

Why is turbocharged transformation necessary?

Beyond conventional ideas of change management, accelerated transformation is a concept. It represents an all-encompassing, integrated strategy that blends operational excellence, strategic insight, and a laser-like concentration on execution. However, why is accelerated transformation so important in the context of modern business? Let's examine the main causes:

Technological Developments Quickly

Technology is changing quickly and causing disruptions in many different businesses. Technologies like blockchain, the Internet of Things, artificial intelligence, and machine learning are not simply catchphrases; they are revolutionizing the way organizations function, compete, and provide value. Businesses that don't adapt to these developments run the danger of becoming obsolete. With the help of enhanced productivity, new value propositions, and the incorporation of cutting-edge technology into your company model, turbocharged transformation makes sure you remain ahead of the curve.

Higher Expectations from Consumers

Consumers nowadays are more knowledgeable, connected, and powerful than in the past. They want frictionless interactions across all touchpoints, rapid satisfaction, and tailored experiences. In order to foster customer loyalty and promote expansion, businesses need to react quickly to these changing demands. You can use data analytics and customer insights to offer exceptional experiences that thrill and engage your consumers, resulting in long-term connections and brand advocacy with a supercharged transformation.

Global Competition Intensified

Many sectors now have fewer entry barriers, which has resulted in an invasion of global rivals. Businesses need to set themselves apart from the competition by being more innovative, flexible, and well-executed. By using a turbocharged transformation strategy, you may outperform rivals by streamlining your business processes, launching new goods and services quickly, and making constant improvements to your current offers.

Volatility and Uncertainty in the Economy

Volatility and uncertainty are hallmarks of the global economy, since shifts in market conditions, geopolitical conflicts, and unanticipated catastrophes such as pandemics greatly affect company operations. For businesses to effectively handle these hurdles, they need to be robust and adaptive. With the help of turbocharged transformation, you can create an adaptable and strong company that can quickly adapt to changing conditions and maintain continuity and development.

Compliance and Regulation Pressures

With new rules and regulations arising across sectors and geographical areas, the regulatory environment has become more complicated. Compliance now demands proactive management and integration with corporate operations; it is no longer only a box-ticking activity. Reducing risks and improving your reputation, a supercharged transformation framework helps you remain compliant by integrating regulatory concerns into your operational execution and strategic planning.

Social Responsibility and Sustainability

The role that sustainability and social responsibility play in fostering company success is becoming more apparent. Businesses that exhibit a dedication to social impact, ethical business practices, and environmental sustainability are gaining importance from stakeholders, investors, and customers alike. By incorporating sustainability into the heart of your company strategy, turbocharged transformation enables you to generate long-term profit while making a beneficial impact on the environment and society.

Accepting the Trip

Starting a supercharged transformation journey requires a basic change in perspective and strategy. It entails dismantling organizational silos, encouraging teamwork, and developing an innovative and adaptable culture. It requires a commitment to experimentation, learning, and iteration, along with a persistent concentration on execution. Above all, it needs inspiring and motivating visionary leadership that can unite the whole firm around a common objective of faster development and success.

We will provide you with the knowledge, resources, and techniques you need to successfully traverse this life-changing journey in this book. We will assist you at every stage of the process, from evaluating your existing situation to establishing challenging but doable objectives to developing a solid plan and carrying it out to the highest standard. With the help of applicable examples, useful guidance, and workable frameworks, you will acquire the skills and self-assurance necessary to take your company to new heights.

Greetings from the new age of expansion. Welcome to change with a boost. Together, we can hasten your path to achievement.

CHAPTER 1: ESTABLISHING THE BASE

Setting off on an accelerated transformation journey requires a solid base. This entails knowing how development works, evaluating yourself truthfully at this moment, and establishing challenging yet doable objectives. Let's examine each of these crucial areas to make sure your company is ready for quick and long-term success.

Comprehending Growth Dynamics

Growth is a journey rather than a destination, requiring a strategic attitude and a clear grasp of the variables that propel progress. The growth mentality and important forces for company development are examined in this section.

The Mentality of Growth

The idea that skills and intellect can be developed with commitment, effort, and the appropriate techniques is known as a growth mindset. Psychologist Carol Dweck popularized this idea, which is crucial for people and organizations seeking long-term progress. A growth mindset in business refers to being receptive to new ideas, ready to take measured risks, and dedicated to continuous learning and development.

1. **Take on Challenges:** See obstacles as chances to improve and gain knowledge. Urge the members of your team to take on new tasks and ventures outside of their comfort zones.

2. **Learn from Failure:** Recognize that experiencing failure is a normal aspect of personal development. Examine failures to glean important lessons, then use these understandings in your next ventures.
3. **Promote Curiosity and Innovation:** Establish a setting that encourages both of these traits. Encourage staff members to try out novel concepts and strategies without worrying about the consequences.
4. **Continuous Learning and Development:** Make an investment in your team's ongoing education and growth. Offer chances for education, training, and skill development.

Principal Forces Behind Business Growth

It is easier to strategically allocate your time and resources to areas that will provide the greatest returns when you are aware of the main forces behind company development. The following are the main factors to think about:

1. **Market Demand:** It's critical to recognize and address market demand. Identify consumer preferences and wants via market research, then create goods and services to satisfy these needs.
2. **Innovation:** One of the main forces behind growth is innovation. Make research and development investments to produce innovative goods, services, or procedures that set your company apart from rivals.
3. **Operational Efficiency:** Growth may be greatly impacted by streamlining operations to cut expenses and increase efficiency. To increase productivity, use

technology, automation, and lean procedures.

4. **Customer Experience:** Creating a memorable experience for customers may encourage word-of-mouth recommendations and loyalty. Prioritize comprehending client journeys and providing value at each touchpoint.

5. **Strategic Partnerships:** Establishing partnerships and alliances may lead to the opening of new markets and business prospects. Work together with other companies to make use of complementary resources and capabilities.

6. **Scalable Infrastructure:** Make sure your system is capable of expanding with your business. Invest in technology, methods, and procedures that are scalable so they

can accommodate growth in demand without sacrificing quality.

Evaluating Your Present Situation

It's crucial to comprehend where you are right now before setting out on a development path. This entails benchmarking against rivals and doing a SWOT analysis.

SWOT Analysis: Opportunities, Weaknesses, Threats, and Strengths

A strategic planning technique called a SWOT analysis is used to determine both external opportunities and threats as well as internal strengths and weaknesses. This thorough evaluation gives you a clear view of your company's current state and future potential.

1. **Strengths:** Determine the special advantages of your company. These might be resources, skills, or assets that give you a competitive edge. A powerful brand, a devoted following of clients, exclusive technology, or extraordinary talent are a few examples.
2. **Weaknesses:** Identify the areas in which your company is lacking. If you don't work on these shortcomings, they might impede your progress. Limited resources, out-of-date technology, and talent deficits are common drawbacks.
3. **Opportunities:** Seek out outside chances that may encourage expansion. These might be shifts in customer behavior, new technology, or market movements. Finding possibilities enables you to take advantage of them before your rivals do.

4. **Threats:** Recognize any dangers that can adversely affect your company. These might include changes in regulations, pressure from the competition, or economic downturns. You may create measures to lessen the effect of dangers by having a thorough understanding of them.

Comparison Benchmarking with Rivals

Comparing your company's performance to rivals' or the industry's norms is known as benchmarking. You may learn more about your place in the market and pinpoint opportunities for development with the aid of this procedure.

1. **Identify Key Metrics:** Ascertain which KPIs (key performance indicators) are most relevant to your company and sector. Market share, customer happiness, profit

margins, and revenue growth are examples of common measures.

2. **Collect Data:** Compile information on the performance of your rivals. Public financial accounts, industry publications, and market research may all provide this information.

3. **Analyze Comparisons:** Examine how you stack up versus the competition to find weaknesses and opportunities for improvement. Seek out trends and patterns that might help you make smart choices.

4. **Set Improvement Targets:** Determine precise, quantifiable goals for improvement based on your findings. Create action plans to reduce performance gaps and take advantage of your competitive advantages.

Establishing High Yet Achievable Objectives

Establishing attainable, ambitious, and well-defined objectives is essential to promoting progress. These objectives should be in line with your team's broader vision and purpose to provide them with guidance and inspiration.

Outlining Specific Goals

Well-defined goals provide a path for your personal development. They need to be SMART goals—specific, measurable, realistic, pertinent, and time-bound.

1. **Specific:** Specify exact and well-defined goals. As an alternative to general objectives like "increase sales," establish more precise goals like "increase sales by 20% in the next 12 months."

2. **Measurable:** Make sure your goals are quantifiable. This enables you to monitor progress and modify tactics as necessary. For instance, "increase website traffic by 30% through SEO and content marketing."
3. **Achievable:** Establish reasonable goals that are difficult yet doable. When defining objectives, take into account your talents, resources, and the state of the market.
4. **Important:** Match your goals to your overarching company plan and top priorities. Every objective ought to support your purpose and long-term vision.
5. **Time-bound:** Establish a precise deadline for accomplishing your goals. This instills

a feeling of urgency and keeps your group responsible and focused.

Synchronizing Objectives with the Vision and Mission

To ensure that every effort supports your overall purpose and direction, your objectives should be in line with your company's vision and mission.

1. **Revisit Your Vision and Mission:** To begin, go back over the mission and vision statements for your business. Whereas your mission statement explains your purpose and how you plan to accomplish your vision, your vision statement reveals your long-term goals.
2. Make sure your objectives align with your vision and purpose by making sure they are consistent. Each goal should take you

one step closer to achieving your purpose and realizing your vision.

3. **Speak clearly:** Make sure everyone in your company understands your objectives, vision, and purpose. Make sure that everyone is aware of the broad picture and how their specific jobs fit into the overarching goals.

4. **Promote Alignment:** Encourage alignment by having your team participate in the process of creating goals. To make sure that the objectives are reasonable and that everyone is dedicated to reaching them, solicit suggestions and criticism.

5. **Monitor and adjust:** Track your progress toward your objectives on a regular basis and make necessary modifications. To keep in line with your vision and objectives, maintain your flexibility and

be willing to change directions when needed.

Final Thoughts

Successful rapid change requires laying a solid foundation. You may position your company for quick and long-term success by comprehending the mechanics of development, properly evaluating where you are now, and establishing high but doable objectives. This foundation gives your team confidence and inspiration, encouraging them to accept change and pursue greatness while also offering direction and clarity.

Building upon this basis, we will examine strategic planning, excellence in execution, and success measurement as we go through the book. We will work together to negotiate the challenges of business transformation, giving you the knowledge and skills you need to take your company to new heights. Greetings from the supercharged transformation journey. Together, we can propel your development and accomplish remarkable triumphs.

CHAPTER 2: STRATEGIC PLANNING

The roadmap that directs the evolution of your firm is called strategic planning. To guarantee sustainable development, a strong plan must be crafted, resources must be allocated wisely, and risks must be managed. This section of the book explores the nuances of strategic planning and offers a comprehensive guide to assist you in navigating this important stage.

Formulating a Sturdy Plan

A strong plan is the cornerstone of all you do in business. It lays out your goals, your vision, and the precise measures that must be taken to get there.

Developing an All-Inclusive Business Plan

A thorough company strategy is necessary to direct your strategic endeavors. It serves as a road map, outlining the goals, tactics, market research, and financial forecasts for your company.

1. **Executive Summary:** Summarize your business plan's main ideas in a concise executive summary. It should include a succinct synopsis of your company, its objectives, and its strategy for achieving them. Since it establishes the tone for the whole strategy, this piece needs to be interesting and captivating.

2. **Business Description:** Describe your company's nature, including its goals, objectives, and purpose. Give a brief description of your goods and services,

the issues they resolve, and the demands the market has. Emphasize your USP, or unique selling proposition, and what makes you stand out from the competition.

3. **Market study:** To comprehend the competitive landscape, target market, and industrial landscape, conduct a comprehensive market study. Provide details on the market's size, growth patterns, clientele, and main rivals. Utilize statistics and facts to back up your conclusions.

4. **Organization and Management:** Describe the major team members' roles and duties as well as the organizational structure of your company. Provide a brief bio of your leadership team that highlights

their experience and accomplishments for the company.

5. **Marketing and Sales Strategy:** Explain your plans for attracting and keeping consumers, as well as your marketing and sales techniques. Talk about your ideas for distribution, price, marketing, branding, and positioning. Emphasize any ties or strategic collaborations that can help you in your endeavors.

6. **Product Line or Services:** Give specifics about your offerings, such as features, advantages over competitors, and benefits. Describe your development and manufacturing procedures, and talk about any upcoming service or product launches that you have planned.

7. **Financial predictions:** For the next three to five years, provide your financial

predictions, which should include balance sheets, cash flow statements, and income statements. Provide the assumptions behind your forecasts, and highlight important aspects using charts and graphs. This part should show your company's potential for development and financial stability.

8. **Appendices:** Attach any supporting documentation, technological specifications, market research data, important team member resumes, and legal papers that you feel will strengthen your company strategy.

Combining Creativity with Quickness

Innovation and adaptability are essential elements of a strong strategy in the quickly evolving corporate world of today. They help your company stay competitive, take advantage of new possibilities, and adjust to changes in the market.

1. **Promote an Innovative Culture:** Promote an environment that values experimentation and originality. Encourage staff members to come up with fresh concepts and solutions, and provide them with the tools and encouragement they need to see their ideas through to completion. Put in place procedures that encourage creativity, such as cross-functional teams, innovation laboratories, and frequent brainstorming sessions.
2. **Invest in Research and Development:** Provide funds for R&D to promote ongoing advancements and

game-changing discoveries. Keep up with industry developments and technological breakthroughs to spot future areas for innovation.

3. **Agile Methodologies:** Implement agile techniques to improve the responsiveness and adaptability of your company. Iterative development, frequent feedback loops, and adaptive planning are examples of agile approaches that let you adjust swiftly to changing consumer demands and market conditions.

4. **Collaborate and co-create:** Take part in joint ventures and cooperative projects with clients, associates, and other relevant parties. These partnerships may result in creative fixes and fresh commercial prospects. Use crowdsourcing and open

innovation platforms to access outside knowledge and ideas.

5. **Ongoing Education and Adjustment:** Promote an environment where learning and adjustment are ongoing processes. Encourage staff members to participate in training programs, learn new skills, and stay current on industry trends. Review and modify your strategy often in light of performance indicators and market feedback.

Allocating Resources for Maximum Impact

Allocating resources effectively is essential to carrying out your strategy plan and reaching your development goals. To optimize the effect, it entails managing financial resources and maximizing human capital.

Maximizing Human Resources

Your most precious resource is your people. Attracting, nurturing, and keeping talent is all part of optimizing human capital, as is cultivating a high-performance and engaged culture.

1. **Talent Acquisition:** Use methodical hiring procedures to draw in top candidates. Employ a blend of conventional hiring techniques and cutting-edge strategies, such as employee referral programs and social media recruiting. Make sure that the recruiting procedures you use support diversity and are inclusive.
2. **Employee Development:** Make a commitment to your staff members' ongoing professional growth. Provide

professional development opportunities, career growth routes, and training programs. Motivate staff members to get more training and credentials.

3. **Performance Management:** Put in place a strong system for managing performance in order to define goals clearly, provide frequent feedback, and honor and reward accomplishments. To identify strong performers and areas for development, use analytics and performance indicators.

4. **Employee Engagement:** Encourage a motivated and engaged work environment. Promote open communication, provide staff members with a voice and opportunity for engagement, and cultivate a happy workplace. To determine satisfaction and

rectify any issues, conduct surveys on employee engagement on a regular basis.

5. **Leadership Development:** By identifying high-potential staff members and offering them leadership development opportunities and training, you may create a pipeline of future leaders. Encourage partnerships between mentors and coaches inside your company.

Money Management and Investing

To ensure long-term survival and maintain development, prudent financial planning and investment are crucial. This includes making wise investment choices, managing financial flow, and creating an efficient budget.

1. **Budgeting:** Create a detailed spending plan that complements your strategic aims and objectives. Keep a close eye on your

budget and make necessary adjustments to reflect shifting objectives or changes in your company environment. Make sure that every department has responsibility and clear fiscal guidelines.

2. **Cash Flow Management:** To support your operations and strategic goals, keep your cash flow in good shape. Keep a careful eye on your cash flow, effectively handle your payables and receivables, and maximize your working capital. To predict future financial demands and make appropriate plans, think about using cash flow forecasting software.

3. **Technology Investment:** Invest money in technologies that will improve your business's competitive edge, customer satisfaction, and operational effectiveness. Prioritize the technological projects that

will have the most effect after evaluating each one's return on investment (ROI).

4. **Strategic Investments:** Put money into ventures like market expansion, new product development, and strategic alliances that foster growth. Before making an investment, do extensive risk evaluations and due diligence.

5. **Cost Management:** Reduce costs without sacrificing performance or quality by putting cost management techniques into effect. Determine cost-saving opportunities in areas like production, overhead, and procurement, then put those ideas into action.

Controlling and Reducing Risks

Navigating uncertainty and protecting your company from possible dangers require effective risk management and mitigation.

Determining Possible Dangers

Finding possible hazards that might have an influence on your company is the first step in risk management. These risks may be linked to strategy, operations, finances, compliance, or external or internal factors.

1. **Strategic Risks:** Shifts in the market, the competitive environment, or industry trends might result in strategic risks. Your long-term objectives and business plan may be impacted by these hazards. Regularly analyze the market and gather competitive insights to detect any strategic hazards.
2. **Operational Risks:** These risks are associated with how your firm runs on a

daily basis. Process inefficiencies, equipment malfunctions, and supply chain interruptions may all result in these hazards. To find operational risks and opportunities for improvement, conduct audits and evaluations on a regular basis.

3. **Financial hazards:** Variations in income, interest rates, and currency exchange rates are examples of financial hazards. To reduce these risks, keep a careful eye on your financial performance and put in place financial controls.

4. **Compliance Risks:** Modifications to laws, rules, or industry standards may result in compliance risks. These hazards may lead to fines, legal repercussions, or harm to one's image. Keep up with regulatory developments and make sure your company's operations adhere to all

applicable rules and laws.

Creating Backup Strategies

Make backup measures to lessen the effects of any hazards that are discovered. The goal of contingency planning is to make sure that your company can keep running efficiently even in the event of unforeseen circumstances.

1. **Risk Assessment:** Evaluate each identified risk's probability and possible consequences. Sort hazards according to their seriousness and potential impact on your company.
2. **Mitigation Strategies:** Create plans to lessen each risk's effects. These tactics may consist of precautionary steps like putting safety procedures in place, switching providers, or getting insurance.

3. **Crisis Management Strategy:** Create a thorough crisis management strategy that specifies what needs to happen in the case of a significant interruption. Action plans for various situations, roles and duties, and communication methods should all be included in this plan.

4. **Company Continuity Plan:** To guarantee that essential company operations can continue both during and after an interruption, develop a business continuity plan. Recovery processes, backup systems, and alternate work schedules should all be part of this strategy.

5. **Regular Review and Update:** To account for changes in your company's operations, risk profile, or business environment, review and update your risk management and backup plans on a regular basis. To

test your ideas and make sure your team is ready, do frequent exercises and simulations.

Final Thoughts

The key to a successful corporate transition is strategic planning. You may set up your company for long-term development and resilience by developing a solid plan, addressing risks proactively, and allocating resources wisely. This all-encompassing strategy makes sure you are ready to take advantage of possibilities for rapid change and successfully negotiate the complexity of the contemporary business environment.

We shall examine execution excellence in the next section of this book, with an emphasis on implementing

implementing technology and digital

transformation, developing company culture and leadership, and developing your plan. When combined, these components will provide you with the knowledge and abilities you need to take your company to new heights. Let's keep moving forward in the direction of exponential expansion and outstanding achievement.

CHAPTER 3: SUPERIOR PERFORMANCE

Where strategy and reality converge is in execution. It's the stage when strategies are implemented, objectives are pursued, and progress is tracked. This section will cover the essential elements of successfully carrying out your plan, such as putting action plans into action, leading with vision, encouraging a culture of continuous improvement, and using technology and digital transformation.

Putting Your Plan into Action

An effective plan is only as good as how it is carried out. To reach your goals, you must translate your strategic ideas into concrete actions and make sure that these steps are carried out as part of your strategy's implementation.

Milestones and Action Plans

The particular actions required to carry out your strategy are described in an action plan. It allocates roles, establishes due dates, and breaks down your objectives into doable tasks.

1. **Define clear activities:** organize your strategy objectives into manageable, distinct activities. Every task needs to have a clear goal and help you get closer to your ultimate goals.
2. **Assign Responsibilities:** Assign a particular person or team to handle each job. Establish clear expectations for their roles and duties to promote ownership and responsibility.

3. **Set Deadlines:** Give each job a reasonable completion date. Establishing deadlines instills a feeling of urgency and keeps the project moving forward.
4. **Identify Milestones:** In your action plan, identify the major turning points that indicate progress. Milestones provide a means of gauging progress and commemorating successes along the route.
5. **Resource Allocation:** Ascertain that every job has the staff, funds, and time required for a successful completion.
6. **Communication Plan:** Create a communication strategy to update all parties involved on the action plan's development. Keeping lines of communication open and providing regular updates are crucial for preserving

alignment and quickly resolving problems.

Traveling and Observing Development

In order to remain on track with your plan and make the required modifications to stay in line with your objectives, it is essential that you keep an eye on your progress.

1. **Performance Metrics:** To gauge advancement, set up key performance indicators (KPIs). KPIs should provide precise, measurable indicators of performance that are in line with your strategic goals.
2. **frequent reviews:** Evaluate your progress in relation to your action plan and milestones by conducting frequent reviews. These evaluations may take place on a weekly, monthly, or quarterly basis,

depending on the project's size and schedule.

3. **Feedback Loops:** Establish feedback loops to collect opinions from stakeholders and team members. These comments might provide insightful information on what's doing well and what needs to be improved.

4. **Changing Direction:** Be ready to modify your plan in light of performance information and feedback. This might include redistributing funds, altering strategies, or redefining objectives.

5. **Problem-Solving:** Quickly resolve any problems or obstacles that crop up. To overcome obstacles and continue the project, instill in your team a problem-solving mentality.

6. **Celebrating Successes:** Acknowledge and honor victories at each turn. Acknowledging successes raises spirits and inspires the group to keep pursuing the ultimate objective.

Organizational Culture and Leadership

Successful strategy execution requires a strong company culture and effective leadership. While a good culture encourages cooperation, creativity, and continual progress, leaders are responsible for inspiring and guiding their staff.

Guiding with a Purpose and Vision

A leader with a clear vision and purpose gives the whole company motivation and guidance.

1. **Clear Vision:** Express a compelling vision that is in line with your strategic objectives. A compelling vision inspires and binds the group together behind a single goal.
2. **Express Goal:** Make certain that the goal of the plan is understood by every member of the organization. Employee commitment and engagement increase when they understand how their job fits into the larger scheme.
3. **Lead by Example:** Set an example for the attitudes and conduct you want from your group. Establishing a culture of responsibility and integrity by setting an example creates a benchmark.
4. **Empowerment:** Give your team members the freedom and authority to decide for themselves and accept responsibility for

their work. Employees with greater empowerment are more inventive and driven.

5. **Inspire and Motivate:** Encourage and uplift your group through supportive, constructive criticism, and good communication. A motivated team produces more and overcomes obstacles with more resiliency.

6. **Adaptive Leadership:** Demonstrate the ability to lead through uncertainty and change. Be adaptable in your thinking and receptive to fresh viewpoints.

Cultivating an Environment of Constant Improvement

Innovation, effectiveness, and long-term success are propelled by a culture of continual development.

1. **Support learning:** Foster an environment in which staff members are motivated to gain new abilities and information. Provide people the chance to pursue professional, academic, and training possibilities.
2. **Feedback Culture:** Create a feedback-rich atmosphere where helpful criticism is often shared. Feedback is not meant to be interpreted as criticism, but rather as a tool for development.
3. **Innovation Mindset:** Promote an innovative attitude by giving credit for experimenting and ingenuity. Establish safe environments where staff members may try and suggest new ideas without worrying about failing.
4. **Process Improvement:** To increase productivity and cut waste, use continuous

process improvement techniques like Six Sigma or Lean.

5. **Recognition and Awards:** Give staff members credit for their efforts and advancements. Recognizing accomplishments encourages further effort and promotes good habits.

6. **Open Communication:** Encourage open lines of communication inside the company at all levels. Honesty and openness foster cooperation and trust.

Digital Transformation and Technology

Success in a company today requires embracing digital transformation and using technology. These components provide a competitive advantage, facilitate innovation, and improve efficiency.

Using Digital Platforms and Tools

Digital platforms and technologies facilitate decision-making, increase collaboration, and expedite processes.

1. **Collaboration platforms:** To improve communication and project management, make use of collaboration platforms such as Asana, Microsoft Teams, or Slack. Teams may remain cohesive and connected even when they are physically apart, thanks to these technologies.
2. **Data Analytics:** Use platforms for data analytics to collect, examine, and decipher data. Making decisions based on data improves accuracy and offers insights into consumer behavior, industry trends, and operational efficiency.

3. **Customer Relationship Management (CRM):** To monitor sales, manage customer interactions, and enhance customer service, use CRM platforms like Salesforce or HubSpot. Using a CRM system encourages customer loyalty and helps you forge closer bonds with your clients.

4. **Enterprise Resource Planning (ERP):** Implement ERP systems to combine and optimize essential corporate operations, including supply chain management, human resources, and finance. An ERP system provides a unified image of the company, which also increases efficiency.

5. **E-commerce Platforms:** Sturdy e-commerce platforms, such as Shopify or Magento, are vital for companies engaged in retail or online sales. These systems

provide seamless management of sales, inventory, and customer relations.

6. **Cybersecurity Measures:** To safeguard your data and digital assets, put robust cybersecurity measures in place. This covers encryption, firewalls, and recurring security audits.

Welcoming AI and Automation

Artificial intelligence (AI) and automation have the potential to drastically increase production, save expenses, and spur innovation.

1. **Process Automation:** Use technologies like robotic process automation (RPA) to automate time-consuming and repetitive operations. Employees may concentrate on more strategic and creative work when there is automation.

2. **AI and Machine Learning:** Utilize AI and machine learning technologies in conjunction to evaluate big datasets, forecast patterns, and enhance operational efficiency. AI is useful for a variety of functions, including fraud detection, client segmentation, and demand forecasting.

3. **Virtual Assistants and Chatbots:** Use virtual assistants and chatbots to improve customer assistance and service. These AI-powered solutions increase customer happiness and productivity by responding instantly and handling common questions.

4. **Predictive Analytics:** Make use of predictive analytics to foresee future developments in the market, client demands, and possible hazards. By taking the initiative, you may remain one step

ahead of the competition and make well-informed judgments.

5. **Internet of Things and Smart Devices:** Gather data in real-time and keep an eye on operations by using the Internet of Things and smart devices. Quality assurance, equipment upkeep, and inventory management are all possible with IoT.

6. Discover how you use augmented reality (AR) and virtual reality (VR) in training, product demos, and customer encounters. Immersion technologies have the potential to improve visualization, learning, and engagement.

Final Thoughts

The secret to converting strategic ideas into observable outcomes is execution excellence.

You can make sure that your efforts are in line with your objectives by putting your plan into action with well-defined action plans, keeping an eye on your progress, and changing course as necessary. By motivating and directing your team, great organizational culture and effective leadership also improve execution. Operating effectively and continually innovating is made possible by embracing digital transformation and using technology.

We will examine evaluating success in the following section of this book, emphasizing the value of performance indicators, feedback systems, and ongoing development. When combined, these components will provide you with the skills and knowledge needed to propel long-term expansion and outstanding achievement. Let's keep moving forward in the direction of unmatched business transformation and execution excellence.

69

CHAPTER 4: ASSESSING ACHIEVEMENT AND EXPANDING

Your path toward strategic transformation ends with assessing performance and getting your company ready for long-term development. This section covers the essentials of performance measurements, keeping the momentum going, and growing your company to new heights.

KPIs and Performance Metrics

Key performance indicators (KPIs) and performance metrics are crucial instruments for assessing the efficacy of your plans and guiding your choices.

Most Important Growth Performance Indicators

KPIs are measurable metrics that assist you in monitoring your strategic objectives' advancement. Selecting the appropriate KPIs is essential for evaluating progress and pinpointing areas in need of development.

1. **Revenue Growth:** One of the most important measures of a company's performance is its revenue growth. Keep track of your total income as well as the revenue from certain services or product lines. Examine patterns and prospective development regions by doing a long-term trend analysis.
2. **Profit Margin:** Keep an eye on your profit margins to make sure your company stays solvent. Understanding cost control

and operational effectiveness may be gained by looking at gross profit margin, operating profit margin, and net profit margin.
3. **Customer Acquisition Cost (CAC):** This metric calculates the price of bringing on a new client. It consists of sales and marketing costs split by the quantity of new clients attracted. Reducing CAC is necessary to increase profitability.
4. Customer lifetime value, or CLV, is an estimate of the total amount of money a customer will make throughout their lifetime. To assess the long-term worth of your client acquisition efforts, compare CLV against CAC.
5. **Churn Rate:** This is the proportion of consumers that discontinue using your service or product after a certain amount

of time. Recurring income and a steady client base are dependent on lowering the churn rate.

6. **Market Share:** Market share shows how your company stands in comparison to its rivals. Growing market share is an indication of successful tactics and expanding market share.

7. **Employee Productivity:** Measures of employee productivity, such as income per worker or production per hour, shed light on the efficacy of the workforce and operational efficiency.

8. **Customer Satisfaction (CSAT):** CSAT ratings indicate how satisfied customers are with your goods or services. They are usually obtained via surveys. Positive word-of-mouth and client loyalty are correlated with high CSAT scores.

9. **Net Promoter Score (NPS):** NPS asks clients whether they would be willing to suggest your company to others in order to determine how loyal they are. Strong brand strength and consumer advocacy are indicated by a high NPS.
10. **Operational Efficiency:** Order fulfillment rate, cycle time, and inventory turnover are examples of metrics that may be used to evaluate the effectiveness of your operations and pinpoint opportunities for development.

Consistent Evaluation and Feedback Cycles

Staying on course and being able to adjust to changing conditions are ensured by routinely evaluating your KPIs and setting up feedback loops.

1. **Monthly and Quarterly Reviews:** Evaluate your progress toward your KPIs by conducting reviews on a monthly and quarterly basis. Make data-driven choices, assess performance, and spot patterns with the help of these reviews.
2. **Performance Dashboards:** Put in place dashboards that provide current information on your KPIs. With dashboards, you can instantly address any concerns and keep an eye on important KPIs.
3. **Feedback Mechanisms:** Set up channels for workers, clients, and stakeholders to provide feedback. Suggestion boxes, focus groups, and surveys may all provide insightful information on what needs to be improved.

4. **Continuous Improvement:** To promote continuous improvement, use performance data and feedback. To make sure your procedures, tactics, and KPIs are still in line with your objectives, periodically evaluate and improve them.

5. **Benchmarking:** To determine how competitive your company is, compare your performance indicators to those of the industry. Best practices and places where you may gain a competitive advantage can be found through benchmarking.

Maintaining Speed

Sustaining momentum and guaranteeing long-term success requires maintaining high performance and making adjustments to changing market circumstances.

Retaining Maximum Effectiveness

A culture of excellence, a driven staff, and strong leadership all work together to produce high performance.

1. **Leadership Commitment:** In addition to inspiring and directing their staff, leaders must continue to be devoted to the strategic goal. Setting a good example by being devoted and resilient in the face of difficulty.
2. **Employee Engagement:** Encourage a high degree of involvement from your staff by giving them the opportunity to develop, acknowledging their accomplishments, and keeping lines of communication open. Employees who are engaged are more inventive, devoted, and productive.

3. **Training and Development:** To keep your personnel knowledgeable and flexible, make regular investments in training and development initiatives. Promote lifelong learning and provide tools for career development.
4. **Performance Incentives:** Use them to encourage staff members and provide recognition to top performers. Rewards schemes, bonuses, and promotions are a few examples of incentives.
5. **Operational Excellence:** By streamlining procedures, getting rid of waste, and using best practices, you may consistently aim for operational excellence. Operational excellence lowers expenses while increasing production.
6. **Customer Focus:** Continue to place a high priority on client loyalty and

satisfaction. Seek out input from customers on a regular basis, respond to issues right away, and develop to satisfy changing demands.

Switching to Meet Changing Demands in the Market

Maintaining pace and staying ahead of the competition requires the capacity to adjust to shifting market circumstances.

1. **Market Intelligence:** Remain up to date on industry advancements, competition activity, and market trends. Make adjustments to your tactics based on changes you foresee using market knowledge.
2. **Agility and Flexibility:** Foster an organizational culture that is both adaptable and agile. Teams should be

encouraged to try out new concepts, make rapid decisions when necessary, and welcome change as a chance for improvement.

3. **Scenario Planning:** Make plans for potential outcomes in the event of varying market circumstances. Create backup plans in case of unforeseen events like technical failures, legislative changes, or economic downturns.

4. **Innovation Pipeline:** To consistently launch new goods, services, and business models, have a strong innovation pipeline. In a changing market, innovation keeps you competitive and relevant.

5. **Strategic Partnerships:** To broaden your horizons, pool resources, and break into untapped markets, form strategic alliances and partnerships. Relationships may

provide chances for cooperation and reciprocal development.

6. **Risk Management:** To recognize, evaluate, and reduce possible hazards, put thorough risk management procedures into action. You can safeguard your company and handle uncertainty with the aid of proactive risk management.

Growing Your Company

In order to sustain long-term development, scaling your company entails growing operations, gaining market share, and developing a scalable infrastructure.

Expansion Strategies

By using expansion tactics, your company may reach new markets, draw in additional clients, and increase sales and profitability.

1. **Market Penetration:** Take a bigger chunk of your current market to increase your market penetration. Enhancing consumer loyalty programs, competitive pricing, and focused marketing efforts may all help accomplish this.
2. **Market Development:** Take your business into new markets or clientele. To find opportunities and modify your products to suit the demands of new markets, do in-depth market research.
3. **Product Diversification:** Expand your portfolio by introducing new goods and services. Diversifying your product line creates fresh growth options and lessens your dependence on a single source of income.
4. **Strategic Acquisitions:** To spur expansion, think about purchasing other

companies. Acquisitions may drive out rivals while opening doors to new talent pools, markets, and technological advancements.

5. **Franchising and Licensing:** To grow your company quickly and with less money out of it, consider franchising or licensing your business strategy. You may expand your brand by using other people's resources and labor via franchising and licensing.

6. **Partnerships and Alliances:** To expand your reach and capabilities, establish strategic alliances and partnerships. Work together to share distribution channels, jointly create goods, or jointly explore new markets with other companies.

Constructing an Expandable Framework

Growth is facilitated by a scalable infrastructure, which guarantees that your company's operations can accommodate rising demand without sacrificing effectiveness or quality.

1. **Sturdy Systems and Procedures:** Put in place solid procedures and systems that can grow with your company. This involves implementing technological solutions such as customer relationship management (CRM) and enterprise resource planning (ERP) systems.
2. **Scalable Technology:** Make an investment in technology that will expand along with your company. For instance, cloud computing provides scalability and flexibility, letting you modify resources in response to demand.

3. **Effective Supply Network:** Create a flexible, adaptable supply network that can change as needs do. This entails using logistics technologies, building trustworthy supplier relationships, and improving inventory management.
4. **Talent Management:** To draw in, nurture, and keep talented workers, establish a scalable talent management plan. This entails building a solid employer brand, paying competitively, and giving employees the chance to advance their careers.
5. **Financial Planning:** Verify that scaling is supported by your financial strategy. This entails obtaining sufficient funds, efficiently handling financial flow, and making plans for future expenditures in expansion.

6. **Quality Control:** As you grow, make sure you continue to provide consistent goods and services by upholding strict standards of quality control. Establish stringent quality assurance procedures, then evaluate and improve them often.

Final Thoughts

The last stages on your path to fast development and strategic change are measuring success and scaling up. You can monitor your progress and make data-driven choices by putting in place efficient performance indicators and KPIs. In order to keep your company robust and competitive, you must continue to operate at a high level and adjust to shifting market circumstances.

Building a scalable infrastructure that enables long-term development, extending operations, and breaking into new markets are all part of scaling your organization. It's possible to attain long-term success and expand your company with the correct plans and facilities in place.

We will discuss the most important lessons learned from each session in the book's conclusion, along with practical advice to help you keep moving in the direction of supercharged change. Let's review the key takeaways and establish the foundation for your continued development and success.

CONCLUSION: THE PROSPECTS FOR INCREASED DEVELOPMENT

As we come to the end of our exploration of the fundamentals of accelerated change, it's critical that we consider our next steps. This book's tactics and insights are meant to provide you with the resources you need to achieve faster development. But the trip doesn't stop here. Since the corporate environment is always changing, staying ahead of the curve requires a dedication to lifelong learning and adaptability.

Keeping Up with the Trends

Today's business environment is defined by quickening technical progress, changing customer expectations, and altering market dynamics. Businesses need to be proactive, inventive, and flexible in order to remain ahead of the curve.

1. **Acknowledge Technological Progress:** One of the main forces behind faster development is technology. Maintaining a competitive edge requires the constant adoption and integration of new technology that may boost productivity, elevate the customer experience, and spur innovation. This entails making use of blockchain technology, big data analytics, machine learning, and artificial intelligence. You may gain a competitive advantage by keeping up with technological advancements and implementing them into your company plan.

2. **Promote an Innovative Culture:** Your company strategy should be centered on innovation. Promote an environment where fresh perspectives are valued and staff members are inspired to think imaginatively. This entails funding R&D, encouraging an entrepreneurial mindset, and being prepared to accept measured risks. In addition to stimulating development, an inventive culture draws top talent and increases employee engagement.
3. **Remain client-centric:** To remain ahead, it's essential to comprehend and anticipate client demands. Utilize data analytics and consumer insights to customize your goods and services to satisfy changing market needs. Use a variety of methods to interact with your clients and get their

input, so you can keep improving your products and services. Long-term profitability and greater client loyalty may result from developing deep bonds and trust.

4. **Agility and Flexibility:** Keeping the momentum going requires the capacity to adjust to changes quickly. Create adaptable plans that enable quick changes in reaction to unforeseen obstacles or changes in the industry. Motivate your teams to use agile approaches in order to facilitate prompt decision-making and effective execution. Maintaining adaptability in operations, product development, and marketing tactics helps your company stay strong and agile.

5. **Strategic Foresight:** Spend money on foresight-related tasks, including horizon

scanning, trend research, and scenario preparation. These exercises assist you in foreseeing possible future events and making appropriate preparations. You may create plans to seize opportunities and reduce risks by spotting new trends and possible disruptions. Having strategic foresight makes sure that your company continues to be proactive as opposed to reactive.

6. **Sustainable Practices:** It's essential, not merely trendy, to include sustainability into your company's strategy. Investors and customers are giving more weight to companies that practice social and environmental responsibility. Using sustainable methods may save expenses, improve company recognition, and provide new market possibilities. Make an

effort to reduce your impact on the environment, support moral behavior, and improve society.

The Ongoing Process of Metamorphosis

Transformation is a continuous process rather than a one-time occurrence. It necessitates an attitude of constant learning, adaptability, and progress. The following are important ideas to keep in mind as you go on your journey:

1. **Dedication to Lifelong Learning:** Promote an ongoing learning environment in your company. Give staff members the chance to grow professionally, learn new skills, and stay current on industry trends. Your workers will stay informed and flexible in a fast-changing environment if they engage in lifelong learning.

2. **Iterative Improvement:** Approach improvement in an iterative manner. Review your performance measurements, procedures, and tactics on a regular basis to find areas that might need improvement. Apply changes gradually, evaluate their effects, and make adjustments in response to input and outcomes. With this strategy, you may gradually but significantly improve over time.

3. **Cultivate Resilience:** Navigating the ambiguities and difficulties that accompany change requires resilience-building. Create plans to control risks, react to unforeseen events, and bounce back from failures. A company that is resilient can endure shocks and come out stronger after facing challenges.

4. **Involve Stakeholders:** Workers, clients, partners, and investors are among the stakeholders that transformation includes. Engage them and keep them updated on your plans, objectives, and advancements. Encourage cooperation and openness to earn their support and develop trust. Positive contributions to your transformation initiatives are more likely to come from engaged stakeholders.

5. **Assess and Celebrate Success:** Continually assess your performance in relation to your objectives and key performance indicators. Reward accomplishments and significant anniversaries to maintain a good attitude and encourage constructive conduct. Acknowledging successes increases

motivation and motivates people to keep working toward change.

6. **Maintain Momentum:** Long-term success depends on maintaining momentum. Always be looking for ways to innovate and expand. Challenge the status quo and aim for excellence in every facet of your organization to avoid becoming complacent. Maintaining momentum requires a proactive, visionary strategy.

Final Reflections

The capacity to remain ahead of the curve and welcome the never-ending road of change is what will enable faster development in the future. Your company may succeed over the long term by using technology, creating an innovative culture, prioritizing the needs of the client, and being flexible in the face of market changes.

Recall that change is a continuous process. It calls for tenacity, perseverance, and an openness to change. Accept the voyage with an optimistic outlook and an open mind. The tactics and ideas in this book are supposed to serve as a guide, but how well and regularly you use them is what will really matter.

As you go, maintain a clear vision, lofty objectives, and unrelenting work. Accelerated development is a difficult but very rewarding road. You can drive your company to new heights and leave a lasting impression on your industry by being committed to innovation and continual development.

We appreciate you coming along for the ride. We hope your journey toward expedited growth and supercharged change is filled with success. The opportunities in the bright future seem limitless. Accept the challenge and set off on your trip.

www.ingramcontent.com/pod-product-compliance
Lightning Source LLC
Chambersburg PA
CBHW070113230526
45472CB00004B/1239